God Loves Protecting

Inspired by Psalm 91

¹ Whoever dwells in the shelter of the Most-High
will rest in the shadow of the Almighty.
² I will say of the LORD, "He is my refuge and my fortress,
my God, in whom I trust."

Copyright Megan Reda © All rights reserved.

ISBN: 978-0-6488386-8-5

For more books in the GOD LOVES series visit
www.meganreda.com

God Loves Protecting
is dedicated to:

Ollie
Willow
Daisy
Samson
&
Ivy

Thank you for reading God Loves Protecting.

I wanted to write about how God loves protecting because as a little child I was scared of the dark and I know just how important it is to let go of fears and trust God. As you read this book, I pray that the story will bring peace and security and you will learn that no matter where you go God and His angels are only ever a prayer away.

Love Megan x

God loves protecting
Yes! It's true –
God loves protecting
me and you!

God is SO BIG!
BIGGER than the sky –
BIGGER than the mountains
way up high.

BIGGER than the earth
the moon and the stars -
BIGGER than the planets
from the sun to mars.

BIGGER than the ocean
as far as can be -
God is everywhere
If you look - you'll see.

So when it is dark
and things give you a scare -
Know in your heart
that God is there!

Nothing can harm you
in the day or the night -
Even when scary things
give you a fright!

No! No! No!
God WILL protect you –
Angels will come
to stand all around you!

God's Mighty Angels
ready at hand -
To come to your rescue
at God's command.

God will protect you
with His shield and sword -
It comes in the form
of His POWERFUL WORD!

Because you have trusted
in God and His Word –
The sound of your prayers
God's ears have heard.

God will be before you
wherever you go -
Every step that you take
whether fast or slow.

The ground where you walk
Is blessed with great favour -
God is well pleased
with your obedient behaviour.

God's arms wrap around you
in sheer delight -
There is nothing to fear
God's made it ALL right.

Know that God's LOVE
is BIGGER than your fear –
God's LOVE is forever
Every day and every year.

God is SO MIGHTY
and POWERFUL you'll see -
He'll defeat all the baddies
for your VICTORY!

Because -

God loves protecting
Yes! It's true -
God loves protecting
me and you!

www.ingramcontent.com/pod-product-compliance
Lightning Source LLC
LaVergne TN
LVRC091352060526
838200LV00035B/497